iMath Readers

Seeing Halves:
Symmetry in Our World

by John Perritano

Content Consultant
David T. Hughes
Mathematics Curriculum Specialist

NORWOOD HOUSE PRESS
Chicago, IL

Norwood House Press
PO Box 316598
Chicago, IL 60631

For information regarding Norwood House Press, please visit our website at
www.norwoodhousepress.com or call 866-565-2900.

Special thanks to: Heidi Doyle
Production Management: Six Red Marbles
Editors: Linda Bullock and Kendra Muntz
Printed in Heshan City, Guangdong, China. 208N—012013

Library of Congress Cataloging–in-Publication Data

Perritano, John.

   Seeing halves: symmetry in our world/by John Perritano; content
   consultant, David Hughes, mathematics curriculum specialist.
   p. cm.—(iMath)

   Audience: 8–10.
   Audience: Grade 4 to 6.

   Summary: "The mathematical concepts of lines of symmetry and rotational
   symmetry are introduced as a family explores symmetry in objects, animals,
   and nature. Readers learn to identify directions of lines of symmetry,
   multiples lines of symmetry, and congruent shapes. This book includes a
   discover activity, a connection to history, and a mathematical vocabulary
   introduction"—Provided by publisher.

   Includes bibliographical references and index.

ISBN 978-1-59953-564-7 (library edition: alk. paper)
ISBN 978-1-60357-533-1 (ebook)

1. Fractions—Juvenile literature. I. Title.

QA117.P387 2013
513.2'6—dc23
2012034235

CONTENTS

Note to Caregivers:

Throughout this book, many questions are posed to the reader. Some are open-ended and ask what the reader thinks. Discuss these questions with your child and guide him or her in thinking through the possible answers and outcomes. There are also questions posed which have a specific answer. Encourage your child to read through the text to determine the correct answer. Most importantly, encourage answers grounded in reality while also allowing imaginations to soar. Information to help support you as you share the book with your child is provided in the back in the **Additional Notes** section.

Bold words are defined in the glossary in the back of the book.

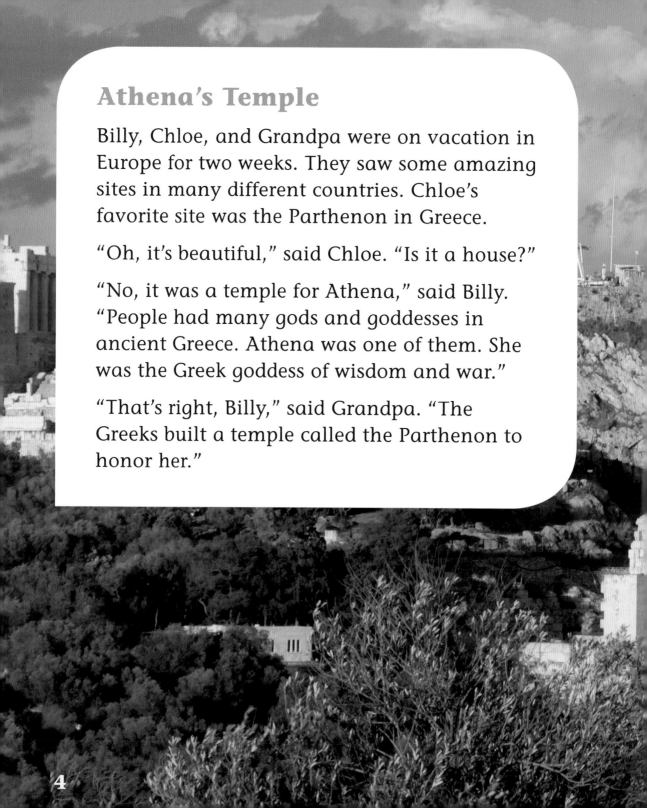

Athena's Temple

Billy, Chloe, and Grandpa were on vacation in Europe for two weeks. They saw some amazing sites in many different countries. Chloe's favorite site was the Parthenon in Greece.

"Oh, it's beautiful," said Chloe. "Is it a house?"

"No, it was a temple for Athena," said Billy. "People had many gods and goddesses in ancient Greece. Athena was one of them. She was the Greek goddess of wisdom and war."

"That's right, Billy," said Grandpa. "The Greeks built a temple called the Parthenon to honor her."

Building Symmetry

Grandpa explained further. "The Parthenon was built about 2,500 years ago. It took eight or nine years to build."

"Imagine the Parthenon when it was first built," said Grandpa. "It must have been even more beautiful than it is today. It was perfectly **symmetrical**, too. When something is symmetrical, you can draw an imaginary line down or across it. This line is called a **line of symmetry**. Two halves on either side of the line are **congruent**. That means that they are the same size and shape. There are many ways to tell if something is symmetrical."

Idea 1: Identify Lines of Symmetry. "To decide if something has symmetry, ask yourself: Does the object have an imaginary line that cuts it into two parts? Are the parts congruent? If both answers are yes, the object has line symmetry."

Idea 2: Identify the Directions of Lines of Symmetry. "Now ask yourself another question," Grandpa said. "If an object has a line of symmetry, what direction is it in? Lines of symmetry can be **vertical**. Vertical lines are straight up and down. They can be **horizontal**. Horizontal lines go side to side. Lines of symmetry can even be **diagonal**. Diagonal lines are slanted and go from the top of one side to the bottom of another."

"There are lines of symmetry on the beach umbrellas at our hotel, right, Grandpa?" Chloe asked.

"Yes, and like the umbrellas, lines of symmetry can go in all directions."

Idea 3: Identify Multiple Lines of Symmetry.

Grandpa continued. "Some objects have more than one line of symmetry," he said. "Think about the beach umbrellas again. They have more than one line of symmetry."

This chart shows other examples of lines of symmetry.

Shape	Number of Lines of Symmetry
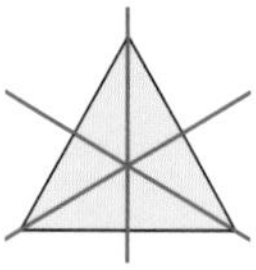	An **equilateral triangle** has three lines of symmetry.
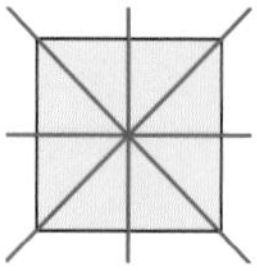	A **square** has four lines of symmetry.
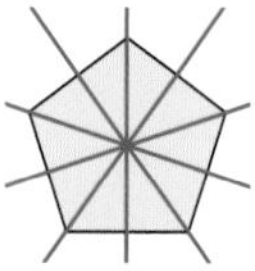	A regular **pentagon** has five lines of symmetry.
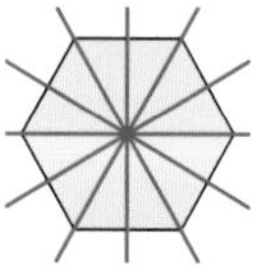	A regular **hexagon** has six lines of symmetry.
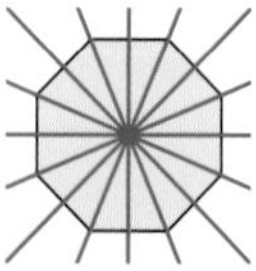	A regular **octagon** has eight lines of symmetry.

Idea 4: Identify Rotational Symmetry. "Some figures have **rotational symmetry**," Grandpa said. "You can rotate, or turn, the figure less than 360° around a point. This point is called the **point of rotation**. When you stop rotating the figure, the figure you see still matches the original figure."

"Imagine the head of a pinwheel," Grandpa said. "Let's call the fastener in the middle the point of rotation. Turn the pinwheel one-fourth the way around, or 90°. The new shape looks the same as the original shape. The pinwheel has rotational symmetry."

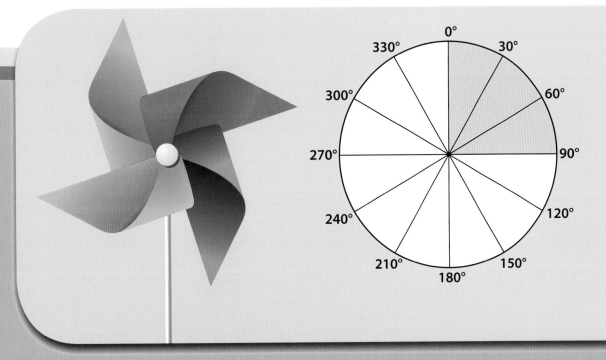

Materials
- paper and pencil
- a ruler or yardstick

Symmetry In and Out

Symmetry is all around you. All you have to do is look for it.

Draw a chart like the one below. Then, look for objects around your house that you think have symmetry. List the objects you find in the chart. You may want to include objects such as furniture. You can include books and TV screens. You can use spoons, forks, and plates. Use any objects you like.

Indoor Object	Does it Have Line Symmetry? (yes or no)	What Kind(s) of Symmetry Does it Have? (vertical, horizontal, diagonal, rotational)

Next, use a ruler or yardstick to determine where the lines of symmetry are on the object. Write your results in the chart.

Now, go outside. Look in your yard or neighborhood. You may be surprised by how much symmetry you see.

Draw a chart like the one below. Then, look for outdoor objects that you think have symmetry. List the objects you find in the chart. You may want to include objects such as flowers, leaves, and trees. Perhaps you see garden beds and sidewalks. There will be doors and windows. You may see some animals, too.

Use your eyes to look for lines of symmetry. Imagine drawing a line on a figure. Then, ask yourself: Are the parts on either side of the line congruent? Does the object have a point of rotation? Write your results in the chart.

Outdoor Object	Does it Have Line Symmetry? (yes or no)	What Kind(s) of Symmetry Does it Have? (vertical, horizontal, diagonal, rotational)

What surprised you the most about what you found?

The Taj Mahal

"Grandpa," Chloe said. "Is the Parthenon the only symmetrical building?"

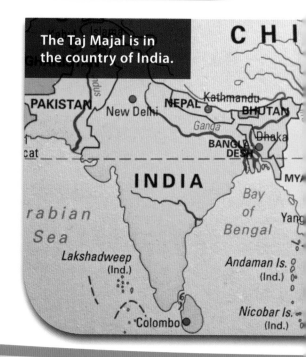

The Taj Majal is in the country of India.

"No, Chloe. Most buildings are symmetrical. But, let me tell you the story of one special building. It's called the Taj Mahal."

Grandpa began his tale.

"Long ago, there lived a prince. His name was Prince Khurram. His name meant 'joyful.' He was the fifth son of Emperor Jahangir. The emperor ruled the country we call India."

"One day, the prince visited the royal palace in Agra. There, he saw a beautiful young woman. She was the granddaughter of a Persian noble. A noble is a person of high rank. "

"It was love at first sight. The prince and princess married. The prince called his love 'Mumtaz Mahal.' That means 'Jewel of the Palace.'"

"The two never parted. The prince led his army in many great battles. The princess was always by his side."

"The prince's father became ill. He made his son Shah Jahan. That means the 'King of the World.' No one had ever been called that before."

"The king died. Shah Jahan became the new ruler. Many people loved him. His people had plenty to eat. They grew rich by selling jewels. Jewels made Shah Jahan wealthy, too."

Look at the photograph of a ruby. This jewel was cut into the shape of a heart. It has one line of symmetry. What kind of line of symmetry is it?

"In 1631, Shah Jahan went to war again. His wife went with him. But during the trip, she became very ill. It made Shah Jahan very sad."

"His wife lay dying. She asked her husband for the most beautiful tomb in the world. A tomb is a place where someone is buried."

"He hired 20,000 workers. They built the tomb called the Taj Mahal. It took them 22 years. The building is perfectly symmetrical. Workers put a minaret, or tower, on each corner. They built a pool of water, too. You can see the reflection of the Taj Mahal in the water."

What kind of symmetry does the Taj Mahal have?

Race for the Tallest Building

"That's a sad story, Grandpa," Chloe said.

"Yes, and it's a true story!" said Grandpa. "Let me tell you another. This one is about two rivals."

New York is called The Empire State. The Empire State Building was named for the state in which it stands.

"Rivals are people who compete against each other. These rivals wanted to build the world's tallest building. In fact, each built two of the most famous buildings in the world."

Grandpa took out his laptop. He pulled up a photograph of the Empire State Building and began telling the story.

"New York is a famous city," he said. "It has many famous buildings. Perhaps the most famous is the Empire State Building. More than 10,000 people visit every day."

"The Empire State Building opened in 1931. It covers an entire city block," explained Grandpa. "It even has its own **zip code** for delivering mail!"

"Builders built $4\frac{1}{2}$ floors each day. It took them less than 14 months to finish the building."

"Go up to the 102nd floor. That puts you 1,250 feet above the ground," said Grandpa. "The building has an antenna, too.

Did You Know?

The Empire State Building has 73 elevators and 6,500 windows. About 15,000 people work in the building. It costs about $4.5 million dollars a year to keep the building lit.

It makes the building even taller. That antenna was a secret until the very end."

"Why?" asked Billy and Chloe at the same time.

"Well," Grandpa explained, "at the time, there was a contest between John J. Raskob and Walter Chrysler. Both wanted to build the world's tallest building. Raskob built the Empire State Building and Chrysler named his building after himself."

"Both men kept their plans secret. Chrysler wanted his building to be the tallest. So, he built a **spire** 185 feet tall. Chrysler was going to put it on top of the building. But, he didn't do that until the very end. He didn't want Raskob to find out and make the Empire State Building taller."

"Workers finished building the Chrysler Building on May 28, 1930. The building stood 1,046 feet tall. That made it the tallest building in the world. But, something happened less than one year later. Workers added an antenna to the Empire State Building. It made the building 1,472 feet tall. The building was hundreds of feet taller than the Chrysler Building!"

"Today, the Chrysler Building is no longer the tallest building in the world. But, both buildings have many lines of symmetry."

"Look at the photograph of the Chrysler Building. How many lines of symmetry does it have? What kinds are they?"

Connecting to History

There are gargoyles near the top of the Chrysler Building. The Chrysler Building's gargoyles are shaped liked hood ornaments, radiator caps, and hubcaps of a Chrysler automobile. Why so many car-themed gargoyles? Walter Chrysler made cars and trucks.

Gargoyles have been around for centuries. Very old gargoyles were found on temple roofs in Egypt. Builders in ancient Egypt used them as water spouts. Water from the roof drained through a gargoyle's mouth. Many times these ancient gargoyles were in the shapes of animals.

In time, builders found other ways to drain water. They didn't need water spouts. So, gargoyles became mostly decorations.

World View

"There are many interesting structures all over the world," said Grandpa. "There are great buildings, statues, and bridges. But not all of them have symmetry."

Look at the photographs. Which of these world structures have vertical lines of symmetry?

A

B

C

D

Math at Work

Architects design many different kinds of structures. They often design structures that have **bilateral symmetry**. The prefix "bi" means "two." A structure with bilateral symmetry has two matching halves.

Daniel Burnham was an architect. He designed the Flatiron Building in New York City. It isn't very tall, but it has an unusual shape. It is shaped like a triangle. The narrowest part of the building is only six feet wide. The Flatiron Building also has a vertical line of symmetry. This line divides the building into two congruent sides. This means that the building has bilateral symmetry.

The Flatiron Building still gets lots of attention. People come from around the world to take a picture of this unique building.

Flatiron Building

Moving Monarchs

"Those are good stories, Grandpa," said Chloe. "But what about living things? Can they be symmetrical?"

"Absolutely," Grandpa said. "Let me tell you about the monarch butterfly. Monarch butterflies like to travel more than we do!"

"Each year, four **generations** of monarchs are born.

The first, second, and third generations live about a month or so."

"The fourth generation is different from the others. These butterflies live longer than the other generations. They also fly south for the winter. They leave North America in the fall before the cold weather sets in. Millions fly to the mountains of Mexico. Others travel to California, Texas, and Florida."

Look at the monarch butterfly in the photograph. What kind of symmetry does it have?

"Some of the butterflies travel up to 3,000 miles. They are the only butterflies that make such a long trip. They'll do it only once."

"Somehow, new monarchs know to follow the same route as their great grandparents. Some even go to the same tree, near milkweed plants. They cover the trees like black and orange holiday ornaments. Scientists do not know why the monarchs migrate to the same place each year."

The wings of a monarch butterfly are congruent. Which shapes below appear to be congruent?

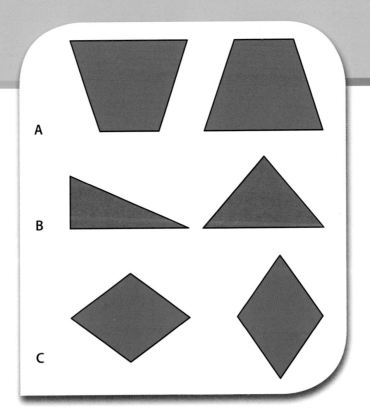

A

B

C

Star of the Sea

"And monarch butterflies aren't the only animals that are symmetrical. Sea stars are, too."

"What's a sea star, Grandpa?" asked Billy.

"It's a starfish. But it's not really a fish. It's an **echinoderm**."

"I know what echinoderms are," Chloe said. "They live in the sea. They have spiny skin. They don't have a backbone. They don't have fins either."

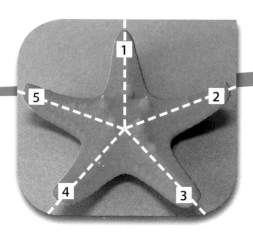

"That's right," Grandpa said. "But let's talk about its symmetry. A sea star has **radial symmetry**. That means its body is like a bicycle wheel. Its arms are called rays. These rays are like the spokes on a bike coming out of the center of the wheel."

"Most sea stars have five lines of symmetry."

"Did you know that sea stars have tube feet?" Grandpa asked.

"Really?" Chloe said with surprise. "What are those?"

"They have a small place on their bodies that lets sea water come in. The water goes into a system of canals, or waterways, in the body. It flows to the tube feet in the rays. When water leaves the tubes, there is a kind of pulling action called suction. This lets the sea star hang onto rocks, climb, or hold its food. Alone, a tube foot isn't very strong. But all together, the tube feet make a sea star very strong."

Sea stars can see, but not the same way we do. They have tiny eyespots that pick up light. Some sea stars move toward the light. Others move away from the light.

Find the Symmetry

Sea stars are only one kind of animal with line symmetry. Look at the photographs. Match each photograph to its related lines of symmetry.

1. Vertical line symmetry
2. Horizontal line symmetry
3. Diagonal line symmetry
4. Rotational symmetry

Spider

Window Blind

Orange

Leaves

"There are lots of things with symmetry, aren't there?" asked Chloe.

"Yes, there are. But we've overlooked something else that has symmetry. It comes with the cold winter weather. Can you guess what it is?" Grandpa asked.

"Snow!" Chloe and Billy said at the same time.

Grandpa smiled. "Did you know that every snowflake has symmetry? And that it is a hexagon? Snowflakes are born in clouds. Think of a cloud as a collection of water drops. When temperatures cool, liquid drops begin to change into solid form."

"The tiniest amount of water is a water **molecule**. A water molecule is made of even smaller parts. These are called **atoms**. One water molecule has two hydrogen atoms and one oxygen atom."

"As temperatures cool, something happens to the hydrogen atoms. They join hydrogen atoms in other water molecules. As they join, they create an open framework. Think of the framework as a skeleton. The skeleton has six sides, like a hexagon. And, it has symmetry. More water molecules join. They arrange themselves in certain places on the skeleton."

"All snowflakes have six sides and symmetry," Grandpa said. "But they don't look exactly the same. That's because the weather in the clouds is always changing. A single change can cause a snowflake to grow a different way."

"Look at the picture of snowflakes. Can you describe their symmetry?" Grandpa asked.

Idea 1: Chloe said, "I can use a ruler to **identify lines of symmetry**."

"How else can you identify symmetry, Billy?" Grandpa asked.

Idea 2: "I can **identify the directions of lines of symmetry**," Billy answered.

Idea 3: "I can also **identify multiple lines of symmetry**."

Idea 4: "Very good, kids," Grandpa said. "We can also look for **rotational symmetry**. Can each snowflake turn around a central point of rotation? If so, it has rotational symmetry."

What type or types of symmetry do the snowflakes in the picture have?

With Grandpa's help, Chloe and Billy described the symmetry of the snowflakes. Afterward, Grandpa reminded them that no matter where they looked, there is symmetry in the world around them.

WHAT COMES NEXT?

Did you know that all insects have bilateral symmetry? Of course, it's not always easy to see that with only your eyes. Some insects are very small. But you can build a simple lens to see them better. A lens focuses light to make something look larger than it is.

Water makes a good lens. You can make a homemade lens. Get a Styrofoam plate, scissors, plastic wrap and tape, water in a sealed cup or jar, and a water dropper.

1. Ask an adult to help you make a hole in the center of the plate.

2. Cover the hole with plastic wrap.

3. Tape the wrap to the plate.

4. Fill the sealed cup or jar with water.

Take your lens, water, and water dropper into a garden. Look for insects. Use your water dropper to put some water on the plastic wrap. Then, when you see an insect, hold the plate above it. Look at the insect through the water. The insect will look larger. You will be able to see its bilateral symmetry.

GLOSSARY

atoms: the smallest building blocks of all matter.

bilateral symmetry: another name for vertical symmetry in which the line of symmetry is in the up and down position.

congruent: the same shape and size.

diagonal: running from one side to another in a slanting manner.

echinoderm: an ocean animal whose body has radial symmetry.

equilateral triangle: a triangle with all three sides of equal length.

generation: all of those born at about the same time.

hexagon: a polygon with six sides.

horizontal: in a straight-across position.

line of symmetry: an imaginary line that divides a figure into two matching parts.

molecule: the smallest part of a substance like water or air. Molecules are made up of two or more atoms.

octagon: a polygon with eight sides.

pentagon: a polygon with five sides.

point of rotation: the point around which you rotate an object.

radial symmetry: symmetry around a central point of rotation.

rotational symmetry: a figure that can turn, or rotate, less than 360°.

spire: a pyramid structure at the top of a building.

square: a polygon with four sides that are the same length and four right angles.

symmetrical: parts on either side of a central dividing line that are identical to each other.

vertical: in an upright position, or running lengthwise up or down.

zip code: a number that tells where to deliver mail.

FURTHER READING

FICTION
Athena the Wise, by Joan Holub and Suzanne Williams, Aladdin, 2011
NONFICTION
Discovering Starfish, by Lorijo Metz, Powerkids Press, 2011
Modern Buildings: Identifying Bilateral and Rotational Symmetry, by
    Greg Moskal, Rosen Publishing Group, 2004
Seeing Symmetry, by Loreen Leady, Holiday House, 2012

ADDITIONAL NOTES

The page references below provide answers to questions asked throughout the book. Questions whose answers will vary are not addressed.

Page 13: one vertical line of symmetry

Page 14: one vertical line of symmetry

Page 17: one line of symmetry; vertical line symmetry

Page 19: Images C and D have vertical lines of symmetry.

Page 21: The butterfly has one line of vertical symmetry.

Page 22: A and C

Page 25: 1. vertical line symmetry: spider, window blind, leaves, and orange; 2. horizontal line symmetry: window blind and orange; 3. diagonal symmetry: orange; 4. rotational symmetry: orange

Page 28: Each snowflakes has vertical, horizontal and diagonal lines of symmetry. Each also has rotational symmetry.

INDEX

CONTENT CONSULTANT

David T. Hughes

David is an experienced mathematics teacher, writer, presenter, and adviser. He serves as a consultant for the Partnership for Assessment of Readiness for College and Careers. David has also worked as the Senior Program Coordinator for the Charles A. Dana Center at The University of Texas at Austin and was an editor and contributor for the *Mathematics Standards in the Classroom* series.